The Truth About Cremation

The Secrets "They" Don't Want You To Know

Find out how you can make the choices that are right for YOU!

Call our office TODAY!

844-552-6739

Corey Brian Strauch F.H. & Pennsylvania Cremation Services, LLC

Corey Strauch, Supervisor
602 Birch Street
Scranton, PA 18505

Or email

Corey@TheTruthAboutCremation.com

Make your appointment for a FREE CONSULTATION (A $195 value)

Give a gift to your family and to YOURSELF by assuring your arrangements will be made exactly as you want them.

www.TheTruthAboutCremation.com

Copyright © 2014 by Corey Strauch

Published by Corey Brian Strauch F.H. & Pennsylvania Cremation Services, LLC

Printed in the United States of America.

ISBN-13: 978-1505341096

ISBN-10: 1505341094

Additional copies are available at special quantity discounts for bulk purchases for sales promotions, premiums, fundraising, and educational use.

For more information, please contact:

Corey Strauch, 844-552-6739

Contact the author directly at Corey@TheTruthAboutCremation.com

Once again, thank you very much for all your help and communication, we appreciate the service very much. Everyone on your staff has made this a dignified and comforting process.

Sincerely,

Donna Chastain, client

Introduction:
Cremation: Learn The Truth

Ever since I was a young boy, I have been taught that anything worth doing, is worth doing well. That's why I have developed a streamlined process for families facing the difficult and often highly-charged emotional period to be prepared to make the choices with which they will always be satisfied with. This process is my calling card. I know our customers are now seeking a fair, structured environment where they can learn about all of the choices available to them in a simple, comfortable and thoughtful manner. In this era, families facing end of life decisions no longer are interested in complicated, pricey and time consuming meetings. Instead, families want affordable choices and personalized attention. Every family and every loved one is different—it is vitally important to me to be able to help the family learn, make the right decisions and to trust in our company—there is never a high pressure sales pitch. Giving personalized attention and being able to truly remove fears and worry by delivering impeccable service, to every family, every time is how I help families through their loved ones' deaths.

When you are in business for more than 100 years the way our family has been, it's easy to see how your customers' needs change and grow through the years. As a fifth generation funeral services

provider and cremations specialist, I take meeting our changing clients' needs very seriously. I have learned from my father who learned from his father before him that our main focus is to be sure we serve families with utmost dignity, mounting respect and careful consideration all the time providing value at a fair cost. Today, I bring these legacy values to my full-service cremation business.

Over the decades, trends in funeral services have indicated the ebb and flow of exactly how families view the end of life. In the past, our family offered services based on our customers' desires and beliefs—something that continues to change over time. Today, 2014 is no different and we are seeing another shift in what our families want and need—particularly regarding cremation. I have a passion to help with today's changing needs, just as my family demonstrated time and again, and I developed a new cremation specific business to ensure that I may exceed expectations in delivering the highest quality in meeting these wants and needs.

Probably the most significant paradigm shift in recent years is the trend of many Americans moving toward cremation and away from traditional funerals. Like many things in life, we tend to learn behaviors from our parents. However, because cremation was not as popular 20 or 30 years ago, there are many questions and confusion around it. Who can authorize a cremation? Do I need a special power of attorney designated so my wishes are followed? My family is opposed to my being cremated, how can I be sure my wishes will be honored? As I tell my customers, education is key in making sure everything goes as YOU want it. And to be sure it happens, you must have ALL of your wishes recorded properly and held securely so that whomever is responsible for executing your wishes is aware and can access the proper documents when the time comes.

Another aspect I have seen shift over the years is how much a family is involved in the process. Years ago, aside from a few choices, the funeral director took care of everything. Today, family members, including the loved one who has passed, have distinct ideas of how they want things. Every cremation service has hundreds of moving parts. I make it my priority to inform the family of all of the different options available to them and once they have made their decisions, I keep in constant communication with the family to keep them updated on milestones throughout. It's surprising how many families really have no idea of how to successfully move through the advanced planning process. That's why I have created the "Your Cremation-Your Way Plan™" to help to lead the families through the process and communicate often and fully.

I have taken 10 decades of experience accumulated throughout my family and have written this book to help you be fully educated and knowledgeable so that you can make the very best decisions. Even more, I wanted every family to have the information they need to make the necessary preparations and make informed decisions. My family is important to me and I know yours is to you too. In this book, I have given you what you need so that YOU can have the peace of mind that emerges when you have the information you need to prepare.

Chapter 1
What IS Cremation?

Cremation is becoming an increasing popular choice for people who want to plan in advance.

Some people choose cremation because they prefer that the assets they leave behind go to their family members rather than being spent on costly caskets, burial plots and so forth. And others are attracted to the many creative options for their remains that are only available after cremation.

While cremation is an important consideration for anyone planning their arrangements in advance, not everyone understands the actual process of cremation.

Knowing exactly what will happen to your remains is a vital part of deciding whether or not cremation is for you.

What Happens During the Cremation Process

Before the cremation begins, the body is placed in a combustible casket or disposable container. The body may be clothed or unclothed, at the option of the family. Some families or patrons choose to clothe the body is a military uniform or other significant outfit.

Before the cremation begins, a <u>heat resistant</u> metal identification tag is attached to the body to ensure proper identification of the remains at all points in the process.

The casket or container is placed in the cremation chamber where the temperature is raised to between 1400 to 1800 degrees Fahrenheit. After approximately 2 to 2 ½ hours, all organic matter has been consumed by the heat. Only bone fragments remain, along with any melted fragments of metal buttons or surgical implants such as pins or screws. (Note: Pacemakers must be removed prior to cremation. Any gold fillings are lost and distributed in the remains by the heat.)

These bone fragments are then collected and removed from the cremation chamber. These remains are commonly referred to as ashes although they are truly more like granules. Any remaining metal is removed with a magnet. Once the metal has been removed, the bone fragments are pulverized into fine particles.

What happens next is limited only by your imagination...and a few legal regulations that apply in most states.

Chapter 2:
Choosing a Cremation Provider

Here are seven key guidelines you can use to help you select a Cremation Provider to handle your cremation plans.

#1 Choosing Your Crematory Location

When you are considering your options, always select a crematory that accepts visitors and allows for public inspection. We are a company that operates our own onsite, private family-owned crematory—there is no outsourcing—we do it all and have a completely transparent process. If you are denied inspection of any part of the process, find another location. When you choose us, you are welcome to visit our facilities and inspect our operation. Because we have decades of experience in helping families through death, we understand the delicate and important nature of taking care of the family members throughout the process; we want our families to feel 100% comfortable with the process.

#2 Witnessed Cremation

Being able to witness the beginning of the cremation process can offer a sense of closure for some people. If your family desires to be present, be sure this option is offered. We know how important this option is to many families and so we offer witnessed cremations. Many of our families choose this option in place of a service.

#3 References

Just like you would ask for references for a potential employee or care giver, be sure to ask the cremation provider for references. Determine that others have been satisfied with their services before committing to them.

#4 Certified Cremation Operators

When you are contacting providers, always confirm that the people providing the cremation services are qualified providers. Ask if the cremationists have been certified by a recognized organization—we have been certified by Cremation Association of North America If the provider cannot produce credentials, keep looking. When you choose a credentialed provider, you can be sure they have been trained well regarding how to operate the equipment and, most importantly, care for your body and ashes. Ask to see their documents that evidence their certification from Cremation Association of North America.

#5 Policies and Procedures

As a reputable cremation provider, we have written policies and procedures available for your review. When you are choosing a provider, be sure to review their policies to be sure your remains will be treated with dignity and respect as they proceed through the cremation process.

#6 Up Front Pricing

The Federal Trade Commission requires up front pricing for all services available from funeral industry providers. As soon as there is any discussion of prices, can provide you a price list. If the provider doesn't, be sure to ask for one.

#7 Identification and Security

One of the greatest concerns about cremation is that your remains will no longer be identifiable and can be lost or accidentally co-mingled with others' remains. Ask the cremation provider what process they use to track remains through the cremation process and how they verify the identity of the ashes after the cremation. We maintain meticulous logs that document our adherence to their stated policies. What's more, we communicate with the family every step of the process so they can feel secure knowing where their loved one is at all times.

Consider these elements when choosing your cremation provider in Pennsylvania. Our company proudly meets or exceeds all of these points.

- **Reasonable Fees.** Providers guarantee a fee that is in line with acceptable fees in the area
- **Pre-Payment Plans.** Pre-payment plans are available that allow you to lock in a fee and never worry about inflation again
- **Accredited Funding.** Their funding company that will hold your funds in trust has passed thorough inspection and possesses all necessary accreditations
- **Certified Planners.** You have access to *certified* advanced planning partners
- **Flat Fees.** They provide guaranteed flat fees so you don't run into add-on or unexpected fees later on
- **No Hidden Charges.** There are no up-charges or surcharges of any kind
- **Excellent Service.** Staff have a proven track record of serving families' needs in a timely and efficient manner
- **Satisfied Clients.** Clients who have used the provider have given excellent reviews on their services
- **Peace of Mind.** And peace of mind knowing that ALL your information is in one place—all it takes is one phone call to begin the process.

Chapter 3:
Cremation Options for Choosing Your Final Resting Place

One of the great benefits of cremation is the many creative options you and your family have for handling your remains. They can remain in an urn on the fireplace mantle (like we see in so many TV shows) or be scattered from a hot air balloon. There are even options to have your remains become part of a coral reef or made into a gemstone and incorporated into a ring or necklace!

So let's talk about some of your options and then some of the regulations and guidelines you should consider in making the decision.

Creative Disposition Options
Your family has many options for handling your ashes.

Here are a number of options to consider:

- Scattering in a park or other significant natural place

- Scattering at sea

- Incorporating into a coral reef

- Placement in a columbarium or mausoleum

- Scattering in a scattering garden

- Interment in a family burial plot

- Inclusion in a special urn garden

- Transformation into diamonds

- Stored in an urn at home

- Burial on private property (depending on local ordinances)

Let's take a look at what you should know about each option.

Scattering in a Park or Other Significant Natural Place

In your advance planning, you might designate a special place you'd like your family to scatter your ashes. While the location may be significant to you, you may also want to consider whether or not the location is convenient to family members who might want to visit often.

In addition, some family members may be bothered by the idea that they can no longer identify a specific location where you "are," especially if you choose to have your remains scattered over a broad area. This concern can be addressed by selecting a very specific place for your ashes to be placed, or poured out, in your special place.

When selecting a location for your ashes to be scattered, be sure it is located on private property and make certain you acquire the owner's permission to scatter there. In the long term, it also important to consider the likelihood of the owners of the private property possible NOT owning it at some time in the future.

Cremation liberates your options when it comes to your final resting place!

Scattering at Sea
A number of operations offer everything you need to have your remains scattered at sea. Select from a variety of vessels, harbors and services. Your family can choose to be present or to send your ashes out to sea and have the ceremony photographed. Of course, this is certainly easy for a family to do on their own if they live near the sea. Simply search the Internet for "scattering at sea."

Incorporating into a Coral Reef
An organization called Eternal Reefs will incorporate your remains into a concrete memorial reef. A concrete cast is created by mixing the ashes with the concrete. The final cast is submerged in the sea and becomes part of a larger artificial reef. In addition to providing a peaceful resting place, the eternal reef facilitates the growth of new life in the sea.

Scattering in a Scattering Garden
Many cemeteries provide scattering gardens. A scattering garden is an outdoor garden where ashes can be scattered rather than placed in a niche. This

provides the benefit of scattering in an outdoor setting where scattering is permitted and where the family can be sure their ability to visit the site for years to come.

Often individuals whose remains have been scattered in the garden are identified on a special memorial plaque, wall or unique work of art on which the names are inscribed. Some cemeteries also have benches on which a plaque may be attached or a living memorial, such as a tree, where a plaque may be placed in front of it. Some cemeteries offer memorializing an individual with an entry in a Book of Memories or Remembrance located in a chapel or mausoleum on the cemetery grounds.

Placement in an Columbarium or Mausoleum

A **columbarium** is an indoor or outdoor wall, not enclosed in a building, where single niche spaces or family spaces can be selected to hold urns. Niches are recessed compartments enclosed either by glass or by ornamental fronts on which names and dates are engraved.

Columbariums may be an entire building, a room, a wall along a corridor or a series of special alcoves or halls in a mausoleum, chapel, or other buildings located in a cemetery or on other dedicated property. For family members who want to know exactly where to find and visit your remains, a columbarium may be a good choice.

A **mausoleum** is an external free-standing building constructed as a monument enclosing the interment space or burial chamber of a deceased person or persons. Niches are located inside the building and, like a columbarium, are enclosed either by glass or by ornamental front panels with inscriptions.

Interment in a Family Burial Plot

Remains can be interred in a family burial plot just as a casket would be in a traditional burial.

If you already own a burial plot or have a space in a family lot, you may choose to inter the cremation urn there. Cemeteries often permit the interment of the cremated remains of more than one person in a single adult space. Or if you wish to be interred in a family plot, but do not want ground interment, there are monuments available to house the cremated remains.

These special monuments can be used for those who have chosen cremation or in combination with family members who have chosen casketed burial. Grave site committal of the urn is available and some cemeteries require that the urn be placed in an urn vault for interment. There are a wide variety of markers and monuments available but you should check your cemetery's rules before purchasing your memorial. The monument or marker you select will be a lasting genealogical record for the generations of your family and a lasting symbol of the special life you want to remember and commemorate.

Inclusion in a Special Urn Garden

Many cemeteries or memorial parks have areas designated specifically for the interment of cremated remains. These areas are called Urn Gardens and are set aside for those who desire ground or above-ground interment.

Some gardens offer individual urn burial plots that will accommodate a marker. Others offer unmarked areas for interment of the urn, with adjacent walls or sculptures for memorial plaques. Check with your cemetery or memorial park on the types of permanent memorialization they offer for garden interment of cremated remains.

Transformation into Diamonds

Locks of hair or ashes can be made into gemstones and mounted in jewelry settings. The beautiful gems serve as a constant and unique reminder of you to your loved ones and commemorate your unique life.

Stored in an Urn at Home

Some families may want to keep you close to home. Remains can be stored in urns created for the purpose and kept at home.

Burial on Private Property

Many municipalities allow ashes to be buried on private property (depending on local ordinances). For families who know they won't be moving anywhere, this can be a comforting choice, allowing your loved ones to visit your resting place daily. It's like having your very own memorial garden right there at home.

Burial with a Pet or Loved One

Many people refuse to be separated from their loved ones, even in death. Most of the options listed above allow interment with a pet or partner. If you choose to be cremated with a pet, you will have to be cremated in separate locations and then brought together. Reputable crematories will not cremate pets in their facilities.

For more common questions about cremation not covered here, be sure to read the next chapter: "Commonly Asked Questions About Cremation."

Chapter 4:
Commonly Asked Questions
about Cremation

Most People know very little about cremation. Almost everyone considering cremation has the same questions. This chapter answers the most common questions asked about cremation that will help you to make an informed decision.

Do People Choose Cremation to Save Money?

While the cost of simple cremation is about 20-25% of a traditional burial, other factors influence this choice. People who prefer the simplicity of the services or want the flexibility cremation offers choose cremation for reasons other than price.

Who Does My Family Call at Death If I Choose Cremation?

If you arrange "Your Cremation - Your Way™" with our company, your family will place one call to us and we will assist your family. While it is best to plan ahead, if you have not, we can certainly guide you step by step at the time of need.

Do You Need a Casket If You Choose Cremation?

No. There is no requirement for a casket. However, most crematories, including ours, do require the body to be placed in some sort of disposable container that will hold the body during the cremation process.

You can, however, choose a casket suitable for cremation if that is your preference. If you intended to hold traditional viewings, caskets for this purpose can typically be rented.

What Advantage is there to Pre-Paying My Cremation Costs?

Pre-payment gives you two great advantages. First, you can lock in today's prices and be guaranteed that your costs will not go up. Essentially, you are protected from inflation. This means that no further money will be due at the time of the cremation. This advantage prevents your family from having to pay for your last needs and a time when circumstances surrounding your death may have led to economic hardship.

Second, you can feel the security and confidence of having handled your own needs rather than placing the burden on others who will be grieving your loss. This especially applies if you anticipate that no family member will be available to take care of your final arrangements.

Can I Be an Organ Donor and Still Be Cremated?

Yes. Being an organ donor does not mean that you cannot be cremated. Organs for donation are harvested prior to any services or ceremonies.

When After Death Can Cremation Take Place?

Because cremation is an irreversible process and because the process itself will eliminate the ability to determine the cause of death, cremation must be authorized by the coroner or medical examiner. Pennsylvania requires a 24 hours wait period before cremation can take place.

Is Any Preparation Required Prior to Cremation?

Pacemakers and other medical devices must be removed prior to cremation as they have a tendency to explode during the cremation process. Any special jewelry will be destroyed in the combustion process and should be removed.

Why Is It Important to Have a Place to Visit My Remains?

Having a place to visit provides a concrete way to memorialize the deceased. To remember and to be remembered are natural human needs.

In almost every culture, memorializing the dead has been a key component of human history. Psychologists say that remembrance practices serve an important emotional function for survivors by bringing closure and allowing the healing process to begin.

Can My Family Take the Ashes Home?

Yes. Ashes are usually placed in an urn that will fit easily on a mantle or shelf. You can select from a variety of different urns design specifically to hold ashes.

Chapter 5:
Cremation and Traditional Memorial Services

Many individuals or their family members shy away from cremation because they believe if they choose cremation a service won't be possible.

This is absolutely untrue!

You Can Still Have a Traditional Funeral

When you choose cremation you still have the option of a traditional viewing and funeral service if you wish. While our firm does not offers traditional viewing and funeral options; many of our families are interested in a more simple, yet meaningful approach—one that allows the family an opportunity to gather afterwards to remember their loved one. Our specialty is offering a simple, direct cremation with Memorial Services held afterwards.

If you or your family strongly prefers a service inside a church building, you should be aware that some churches require embalming to be performed in order to bring the deceased into the building. This is primarily due to health concerns. If you want your service to be held in a church, check with your church to find out what their policies are. This is one reason more families choose the simpler option of holding a memorial service after the cremation.

When a traditional funeral service is held in the church, after the services, the body is then transported to the crematory, rather than to the graveside. If your family desires to witness the cremation, many crematories will accommodate this request. Viewing the cremation is often a substitute for holding a graveside service.

What If I Oppose Embalming?

Since we do not offer embalming services, your immediate loved ones can gather for a private viewing. The body will be cleaned and appearances made to look natural. Until such a visitation can be scheduled the body will be kept in a temperature controlled facility. Again embalming is not necessary for this type of viewing.

You Can Hold a Memorial Service

Another option for a traditional service to accompany a cremation is a memorial service. Memorial services are essentially the same as traditional funeral services. They key difference is that the body of the deceased is not present—either because it has been cremated or for other reasons.

For example, a gentleman from California passed away while visiting his daughter in Arizona. The family burial plot was in Utah. Rather than ship his body all around the country, the family held a service in Arizona for the grandchildren. The body was then cremated and the remains were shipped to Utah.

The next week they traveled to California where they held a service (no viewing or casket) for friends and extended family. Then the daughter and her mother traveled to Utah where they held a visitation at a funeral home and then a graveside ceremony for additional friends and family in the area.

It is not necessary to have the body (or even the ashes) present in order to hold a service. And when the body is cremated, you have even more options for where the ceremonies can be held...and when.

Why Do I Even Need a Service?

While it may seem more important to save money and get everything "over with," a service can bring important closure for your loved ones and give them the opportunity to say goodbye. In addition, a service gives your family and friends the opportunity to celebrate your life. As they come together, it affords them time to comfort one another and grieve together.

Without such a service, family members and friends often feel alone in dealing with their grief. They may lack a sense of closure and be left with an unsettling feeling they cannot resolve.

Services unite your friends and family so they can support each other, work through their grief and add a sense of reunion and love at the time when they need it the most.

Services do not have to be expensive or elegant. They should be designed to meet the needs of family and friends who want to remember you. In a sense, the gathering together is the most important part...however you choose to do it.

As you read the next chapter, Overcoming Family Objections, keep in mind the important need for closure we've just covered. It will help you in reassuring your family that their important needs can be met, even if you choose cremation.

Chapter 6:
Overcoming Family Objections

While you may prefer cremation, your family members may not be comfortable with the idea. If your family does object to your choice to be cremated, the most important thing to do is to find out *why* they are objecting. They may resist your wishes simply because they believe cremation rules out traditional options...which may not be the case at all.

Here are some common reasons family members object to cremation:

- They want a viewing

- They think cremation means you won't have traditional services

- They don't understand all the options cremation offers

- They have a fundamental problem with cremation

- They have religious issues with cremation

Many of these objections can be easily overcome by providing your family with the correct information.

The sections below will help you educate your family and relieve the consternation they may be feeling about your desire to be cremated.

You can have a viewing.

A simple goodbye without embalming or an elaborate traditional viewing embalming is possible. You just need to decide which you and your family would like to have.

You Can Be Cremated AND Hold Services

As noted in the previous section, a service is still possible. You can be cremated and still have an a service for family.

Cremation Doesn't Mean You Will Be Gone Forever

Many family members don't understand all the options that cremation offers. Popular media showing ashes being scattered to the wind give many people the impression that scattering is the typical method of disposition when someone is cremated.

You loved ones may envision your ashes disappearing into thin air. Imagining this kind of separation and finality can augment their feelings of grief and pain.

You can bring comfort to your loved ones by assuring them that cremation allows them to care for your ashes in ways that may be even more comforting and personal to them than a typical cemetery burial. (See Chapter 2: Options for Handling Your Remains.)

Fundamental Issues with Cremation

In many cases, family members can't really put their finger on what concerns them about cremation. The idea just bothers them. Western culture has a long-standing tradition of viewings, open casket funerals, and graveside ceremonies. The idea of cremation is untraditional. And this can make the idea feel "wrong."

Do your best to educate your family about cremation as you express your personal desires and preferences. Ask questions to discover what you can about their concerns (if they can articulate them) and then do what you can to bring comfort to them.

Some Religions Oppose Cremation

Your family may not want you to be cremated because they have religious objections. While many religions *do* have official positions regarding cremation, sometimes it's more of a traditional or cultural belief than a doctrinal declaration.

If adhering to religious guidelines is important to your kin, do your best to find out what the official stance of your denomination actually is. If your church opposes cremation, then you have a decision to make. On the other hand, if the belief is more of a guideline than a rule, you might be able to use that information to negotiate your desires with your family.

The greatest advantage to letting your family know your wishes *now* is the ability plan your services in advance.

Chapter 7:

Cremation Planning in Advance

Planning your services in advance can be a great advantage to your family. It is difficult when one passes away to bear the burdens required to plan services and make the many decisions that could have (and should have) been made far in advance. You can also pre-pay for your services. However, before you can pre-pay and lock in today's costs, you will need to make a number of decisions that influence what that final cost will be.

Planning In Advance

Planning in advance simplifies the laundry list of choices and offers easy payment options. Just as it is your responsibility to take care of your body in life by washing your hair, brushing your teeth, exercising and taking it to the doctor, it is also your responsibility to take care of your body in death. The fact that you pass away does not relieve you of this responsibility.

If you were to meet with a funeral planner today, here are some of the questions he would ask you:

1. Do you want just a Simple Cremation?

1. Do you want your family to be able to say goodbye before your body is cremated?

    a. In a private setting?

    b. In a public setting like a church or funeral home?

2. Do you want embalming or not?

3. Will your family be able to see you within 24 hours or not?

4. Do you want a service

   Where will the service be held?

   a. Church

   b. Funeral home

   c. In someone's home

   d. Somewhere else

5. What is your preferred disposition of your ashes?

   a. Niche

   b. Columbarium

   c. Burial plot

   d. Scattered

   e. Other

Of course, as you look at the list above, it may seem simplest to be cremated and skip all the details. However, keep in mind that one of the primary objections families have to cremation is their belief that cremation rules out holding the farewell services they so tenderly desire.

To give you an idea of the considerations you must make, let's walk through each of the questions above.

Do You Want Just a Simple Cremation?

A simple creation is our number one specialty. I have created a thoughtful, meaningful approach to allowing your family to grieve without all of the extra costs of a traditional funeral. The body will be transported directly from the place of death to crematory without all of the weighing choices and costs associated with caskets, viewings and services. Once the body has been cremated, the family then can proceed with the Memorial Service they wish in the timing that they choose.

If you aren't leaving behind any family members or friends who will want to grieve your loss, or if you want your family to decide with no guidance from you, cremations planned in advance takes all the decision-making out of your end of life services.

Do You Want Your Family to Be Able to Say Goodbye?

If you want your family to be able to say goodbye, you have many options to choose from.

Say Goodbye in a Private Setting

If you want only your family and closest friends to be able to say goodbye to you, a private setting is usually the best choice. The service is held privately.

Can You Hold the Viewing within 24 Hours?

If you wish to have a viewing so your family can say goodbye, your family will need to hold a viewing within 24 hours or choose refrigeration.

What Type of Service Will You Hold?

If you will hold a service, you will need to decide what type of service it will be. If you want your ashes present for a post-cremation memorial service, you will need to select an urn in which the ashes will be placed. The crematory provides temporary storage urns, but you will most likely want something more elegant for display at the memorial service.

Where Will You Hold the Service?

Where you hold the service will impact your advanced planning and costs. You might hold the service in a church, a social hall, personal residence or other location. Considerations such as transportation costs, facility rentals and such must be planned in advance and paid for in advance.

What Will Be Done with Your Ashes?

Chapter 2 covers a number of options for handling your ashes. Here are a few additional considerations not mentioned before.

If you choose a cemetery plot, local guidelines may require an Urn vault...adding to the cost of the burial.

If you want to be buried with someone or with a pet, some locations may charge additional fees for the additional placement. For example, one man wanted to bury his mother and father together, in one urn, in the family burial plot. The cemetery wanted to charge him an additional $1,000 for the extra ashes even though no additional space would be required!

Be sure to check on your options. Once you have made your decisions in advance, you can then estimate the costs of carrying them out.

Pre-Payment

Most cremation providers offer options for pre-payment of all your cremation needs. The payment is not held by the individual Provider.

All funds collected by me are held in trust by an insurance provider or bank who guarantees the services for which you have pre-paid will be provided at the time of your death.

In order plan in advance and pre-pay your death services, follow these steps:

1. Contact us.
2. Plan your services and calculate the costs to be prepaid. We will document your wishes and give you copies for you family. We always also keep a set on file.
1. Pre-pay for your services either in full or with easy low monthly payments
2. Deliver copies of the vital documentation to your family members so they will know how to take advantage of your advance planning and pre-payment when the time comes.

Note that when you pre-pay, your payment is made out to the insurance company or trust that will be holding and securing your funds. Our company is the only beneficiary named in the policy. They do not receive any payment for future services until services are rendered.

If a service provider asks you to pre-pay for services and make the payment directly to them in *their name*, DO NOT give them any money. This is a red flag indicating potential fraud. Funeral directors have gone to jail for fraud for accepting and misusing funds in exactly this manner.

For information and guidance on selecting a Cremation Provider, see the chapter on Choosing a Cremation Provider.

Chapter 8:
Making The Decision—Is
Cremation for YOU?

Now that you've had time to review all the information in this book, the question you must answer is:

Is cremation for you?

To help you make your decision, here are a few guidelines to assist you.

Cremation is for YOU if...

- You prefer options

- Your family doesn't object

- You prefer less expensive services that cremation provides

- A traditional underground burial unnerves you

- You like the idea of scattering your ashes in a significant place

- Your family tends to move around and wants to take "you" with them

- You're not sure where you'd want to be buried and want to assure the family can be together

- It just feels right to you

Still Have Questions?

If you have read this book and still feel you want to talk further with me, as the owner, I am here to serve your needs and answer your questions.

Contact me today to discuss your custom "Your Cremation-Your Way Plan™".

Visit us online at

www.TheTruthAboutCremation.com

Call me directly at: **844-552-6739.**

OR

Send me an email to:

Corey@TheTruthAboutCremation.com.

I am truly hopeful that I helped reveal all of the truths you need to know when selecting cremation as your family's choice.

Warmest Regards,

Corey Strauch

About the author: Corey Strauch

As a fifth generation funeral services provider, Corey Strauch has developed a passion for helping people experience the calm and dignity of knowing that their future is decided and that it will happen exactly as they desire. Over the years of working with generations of clients, Corey has made it his life's work to help people to be informed, to be prepared, and to feel secure with end of life cremation decisions. This same passion is what has led him to gain the very best education, and ultimately, certification and licensing credentials from Penn State University, Simmons Institute of Funeral Science and Cremation Association of North America. He is a licensed funeral director in Pennsylvania and has garnered 21 years of experience in the funeral and cremation industry. Today, he continues to help people successfully experience security and cutting edge services regarding end of life choices with a legacy that dates back to the early 1900s.

Allow him to assist you in reviewing your options and to set a sturdy and secure plan for your cremation decisions. Learn more about Corey by calling 844-552-6739 or visit **www.TheTruthAboutCremation.com** to find out what your options are and to request a free consultation in order to learn how you can gain the confidence of knowing your affordable plans for cremation are securely set.

Learn MORE about how YOU can make the very best choice for your cremation services.

Call me, Corey Strauch, Supervisor

Pennsylvania Cremation Services, LLC

844-552-6739

OR VISIT us online at:

www.TheTruthAboutCremation.com

OR Clip and Mail This Offer to:

602 Birch Street
Scranton, PA 18505

YES, Contact Me About Cremation Information

*Name:*_____

*Phone:*_____

Make an appointment for YOUR Consultation and I'll waive the $195 fee!

It's completely FREE!

Take care of the <u>most important</u> FINAL decision of your life.

Give a gift to your family and to YOURSELF By assuring your choices will be made exactly as You want them.